Book 1

Montage Through My Eyes

Written By A.S.B.

Art by Victoriia Rusyn

Thank You –

To all those who created the montage of memories I stored away for 10 years.

Able to finally set free:

How I seen you

How I have seen through you

How you all are locked in my heart

& How you all have bloomed in my memories

-A.S.B.

01.09.15

9:59pm

“Can I Kiss You Right Now?”

This interruption is the best one of all.

Of all the sentences I wish to hear on repeat.

Is the one you said right before our first kiss...

12.14.14

12:07pm

1.2.3.

This season I ride the train 3 times,

2 times in 1 day.

You will come home on the last day I ride the train,

1 month, 2 weeks, 3 days.

01.03.16

7:11pm

01.03.16

Getting pushed out early

But maybe I am ready.

The next chapter waiting

But it will not be hate or pity.

It will be soul searching and saving.

It will be shared with Him

Every step of the way.

06.08.16

11:27pm

A Foreshadow Dance

We danced to a paradox

The lyrics not to a love song

Our dance is broken like my heart

Forever clinging and spinning.

Sometimes I think that maybe it was lust for you

I only ever seen you cling to my skin,

Not my soul.

You know nothing about me

But when you felt yourself falling

You pushed me under to drown for you.

06.08.16

11:28pm

A Great Night Sleep

It is best to cry at night.

Before bed.

Because once you're done, your eyes feel clear.

Your ears open, and so you tend to listen.

Some may feel dizzy after a great cry.

Others feel like lungs have been baptized.

But most of all,

Our hearts hurt a little less

And we tend to smile a little more.

So now, go get some rest.

For you sleep greater than other nights

Because your heart can finally catch rhythm again.

11.01.15

8:11pm

A Heart Beats for War

I am searching,

searching for someone.

He is sailing on a boat

to many ports.

Along with weapons

of many sorts.

War is cruel,

War is long,

And so is my heartbeat

for you.

11.01.15

7:59pm

A Hurt Well Shared

I watch my best friend's mother paint a smile on her face.

She doesn't let them see:

The cheating husband

The cancer that is eating him away

The money they are losing

The non-satisfaction of bearing only one child.

She doesn't let them see the regret and hurt flooding her heart.

But I see everything.

Because everything she is living.

I am too.

07.28.16

5:46am

A Trip Paused

This hurts,

Him saying he'd be here and isn't.

I'm torn because

I want to leave without you

But it is your birthday

Should I just go?

Be anonymous to everyone

Dancing alone

Bumming a smoke?

You should be here

And clearly your phone is off for a reason.

You need to be here.

It hurts too much to think of the doubts.

Leaving me in sorrows

Makes my thoughts vine out to only negative conclusions.

06.09.16

12:04am

A True Pianist

I want to learn to play the piano.

Someone buy me a piano;

So it can be untouched to collect dust.

11.01.15

7:51pm

A Walk Down the Street

Something flew

I didn't see it till it hit me.

You smiled as you turned my face towards you

And you laughed at my bad luck

I leaned my face into your warming touch.

All the bad luck in the world fades away

Because I have you.

11.01.15

8:10pm

abcdE.

She plays the game with her eyes and her smile. Loving the attention of many. When one steps out of the crowd, she is taken back. She gets angry, she is always in relations with someone. The man comments on her behavior and shames her for it.

Why do you love the attention and affection?

You have a man,

You have ***many.***

11.01.15

7:43pm

Absolute Infatuation

Your smile can end wars and your laugh can cure cancer.

I could look at that smile forever and stay infinite within your laugh.

06.08.16

11:29pm

Accepting Love

I finally did it.

I accepted it.

Only took me seven thousand,

one hundred,

ninety-five days.

But now that I accept it,

Where is it?

Why has it not come?

Why haven't you?

11.01.15

8:03pm

Act On Impulse

Look at his lips.

Press up against him.

Kiss his neck.

Take his hand

To your chest.

Move towards his lips

While he moves to your hips.

Let him take control.

Let him breathe you in.

11.01.15

8:03pm

Adieu

Each passing moment with you,

Time is slow.

Every look,

Every touch,

Every kiss...

But like Cinderella, I must go

Time snuck up on me,

Because the stroke of midnight is my adieu.

07.28.16

5:05am

Alone

The latest you arrived was near

I am worried you won't come home.

I am afraid to call and get no answer.

Even worse,

I am afraid to call, and you do answer...

And confirm my greatest fear.

I am alone.

But I know you are not.

11.01.15

8:03pm

Always One Step Ahead

Never thought this would have happened to me.

A sailor cheated on me.

He was drunk and I was hurt.

For the night before I had a dream.

A dream that another was locked on his lips.

I was in the doorway frozen,

But you didn't know I was there.

I was a ghost of the past.

Your past.

But there was a second part to this dream.

You and your lover vanished in smoke.

As I turned away from the doorway

I bumped into a man.

I know this man.

He is my temptation.

For I never acted upon,

Until now.

11.01.15

9:01pm

Amazed

I don’t think I could love you more than I do today.

But you always prove me wrong when I love you more than yesterday.

07.28.16

3:54pm

Andrew

I wish my mentality was like yours.

You don't ask questions when you know something is wrong.

You just act accordingly.

You never ask for help.

You always just deal with it.

You don't let the little things get to you.

You don't show too much emotion.

Just annoyance.

You know, I used to be like you.

And I have been struggling

I have been struggling to become that girl again.

Someone who doesn't care as much

Someone who just rolls with the punches.

Someone who knows controlling things that can't be,

is a waste of time.

I was always told to care more and to have a better attitude.

But now, I want to go back.

So much simpler.

So much more I didn't feel.

07.28.16

5:31am

At Fault

I ruin everything.

The way you act out,

The words you say.

All because of me.

12.23.14

9:28pm

B

I sleep with your name

Filling my thoughts,

Across my lips,

In my heart,

And

Between my hips.

05.20.16

12:39pm

Big Gramma

Family is not the same with you gone.

You kept it together.

Holidays are split.

Holidays are short.

The life in the room is removed

And so is my smile.

This is not what I know.

This is now how I grew up.

These gatherings aren't worth it.

I want to stay forever young.

I want to stay forever with you.

How do I bring these memories back to life,

And once more shared with you.

11.01.15

8:04pm

Biology

Your hands are the sun,

My heart is the bud.

You help create photosynthesis

And give me life.

11.01.15

8:05pm

Blinded?..

Always trust your dreams.

Mine was about love cheating on me.

I didn't want to act on it because,

It is just a dream.

But it was his truth.

And a day later he confirmed it.

But I am content.

I guess this warning helped me prepare.

But I don't want to be the one who is content.

I want to lash out but, in my heart, I know I shouldn't.

Is this why they call ones like us,

Blinded?..

11.01.15

7:50pm

Broken Heart

You forever will not be br**ok**en

Because in the middle of it

Everything is **ok**

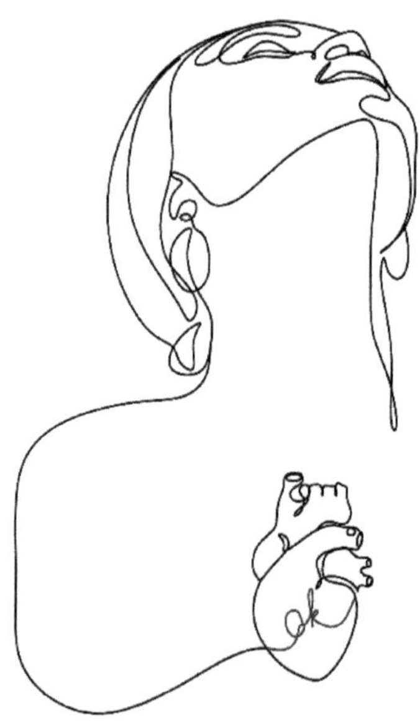

01.26.16

11:32pm

Brooke

You promised her.
Then you broke it.
She cried & whined,
Because it's all about her.

You never told me.
This is the second time
I find from another.
And you are going to leave
Before the birth.

You even dare ask
With questions.
I don't want to speak
To thee for a while,
Possibly ever.
Because you always
Must lean on
Another.

11.01.15

8:39pm

Burst

I hate that I can't stay mad at you.

You didn't tell me that you were still here.

I went two days without talking to you.

It was killing me.

I heard from your mother the day I received your gift.

You were shocked to hear from me.

But I was hurt.

Then you told me why you did it.

Because it was a way for you to make it easier on yourself,

To leave me out of your thoughts,

Even just a day.

So, when you go back,

It didn't hurt as much.

12.14.14

9:33pm

Can't Move On

All I have ever known were your lips.

But I do not want to anymore.

I have seen someone else's that I desire more.

When I left you,

I tried so hard to taste the new.

But the old left me with a wondering heart,

& a filled mind.

12.14.14

8:20pm

Chris

I was told the news today,

I held back tears at how fast your life can just end.

I need you to hold me tonight

But it will have to wait.

So, I cry alone in the silence

And pray in the dark.

06.08.16

11:34pm

Cinderella Story

I don't believe in them.

I am a realist.

But then my gift from you

Made me believe.

You told me it was for

My birth,

My beauty,

And our sacrifice.

I will wait,

Because tonight I can't say no.

I cannot shake those thoughts of you.

Or the thoughts of love.

Who knew someone knowing the game,

Isn't afraid to play.

Because I do have a prince

That isn't just charming.

11.01.15

8:08pm

Clinging To the Body That Is Near

I used to look back on our memories

And smile at the comfort of them.

But every time I pictured your arms around me

I feel you pulling away,

Watching you turn,

You reach for the bottle.

Without any control

It consumes you.

You black out.

Then she emerges from the shadows...

"That's her."

She pulls you in and you cling to her.

Because you can feel her over there

When I am over here.

11.01.15

7:29pm

Constant Love

To be young and in love?

To be in love!

Everyday

Constantly

Never dulling,

never fading.

To hit my heart

With the arrow!

Forever,

Constant,

Love.

11.01.15

8:08pm

Control

Don't let someone control the light in your life.

Because at their will,

They will shut it off.

04.05.16

8:21pm

Crash Into Me

I woke up in the night and traced the outline of your beauty with my fingertips,

Wishing it was with my lips.

And with every trace,

I felt like it was time for our soft skin,

To be broken in.

01.03.16

7:00pm

CS

You deny my love

But you accept the flirtatious side of me.

I ask you why you are like this.

You say this is how you kill

This is how you weave in.

You say you feed on this.

This is how you energize

This is how you breathe.

This is how you think.

Because it's only fair to prepare yourself for only lust.

For it is easier to play

Than to ever feel that way again.

07.28.16

5:43pm

Current Definition of Love

Nothing lasts forever, the pick me ups, the exchanges, the laughter. It's all covered up by the tears and the noise of our voices raising at one another. The love fades as quick as the memory is made. My heart is burning within the same feelings as every other one before you came. And went. When am I ever going to find the one who is going to hurt me less than the last one?

12.16.14

8:48pm

Dear Sailor,

I do trust you,

Just not her.

I do want you,

But so do they.

I do need you,

But our country does too.

I do miss you,

But do you even miss me?

07.28.16

5:35pm

Denied Driver

I'm going to deny you every time

Like how you deny my love.

Nothing hurts more than the one you love

Not wanting you back.

So, the further I drive north

The more south we get.

07.28.16

5:09am

Denied Love

I don’t want you to think I want out.

You are my home, my shelter, my hideaway-

I want you to hear me when I say I never felt this way

I know my actions were wrong

My lights weren’t on.

I was stuck in the thought you denied me of

And it made me feel vulnerable and weak.

12.14.14

9:45pm

Do You?

I, You, & Love

Yes,

I want to.

I want love.

I am ***ready.***

But I sound selfish.

12.16.14

9:35pm

Domanique

It hurts too much to see you.

At a party, in the house, or in the car.

For me, sleep is unsettling.

Because for one more month I sleep next to you.

And for that month I read your dreams,

I know you dream of kissing him

Instead of me.

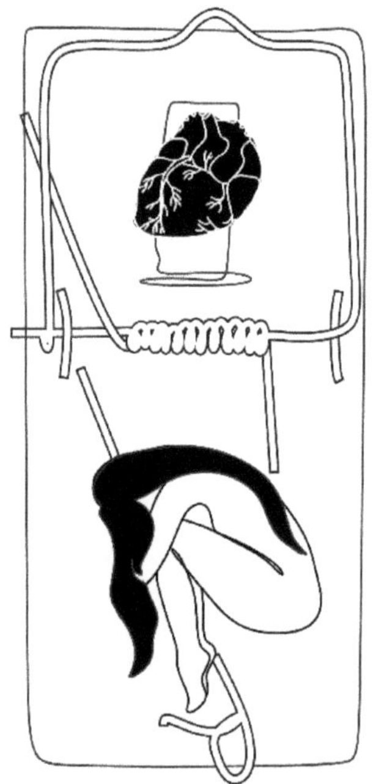

06.08.16

11:37pm

Don't

You asked me what I thought about the song when you played it that night.

I didn't tell you the honest answer.

I thought about myself,

And the other man I was with at the time.

How you are the one singing the lyrics,

Not Bryson Tiller.

You, meaning every word, pouring your heart out to me.

Telling me how blind I am.

That what is true is right in front of me;

That you will take care of me in every way he should be.

I always think back to this night.

The night we stayed out driving around the city till 3am.

At first, I thought it was us catching up,

When in reality, it was us catching feelings.

12.16.14

9:30pm

Don't Be This Dude

For she struggles underneath his breathe.

She feels pain in her wrists.

Something stiff down below.

She begs him to just go.

He stops.

He stares:

At her tears,

At her bruises,

At her breasts.

He proceeds.

11.01.15

8:09pm

Drugged

When you spot it on the neck,

Don't let your voice take full breath.

There can be scary nights we cannot recall.

Due to a drink in a hand that is not yours.

12.14.14

9:49pm

Fears

I only have three fears:

1. The Dark
2. A Broken Heart
3. Loosing You

Funny,

I don't even have you, but I felt all three the day I met you.

11.01.15

8:11pm

Give Into Me

Do you want to be taken over?

Do you want me to be in control?

Just give me your world,

Give into me.

For the night is veiling

And my mouth is watering.

Your neck tastes so sweet.

I know you're not this kind

But I love you this way.

Soft,

Selfish,

Willing.

Give into the night.

Give into me.

07.28.16

5:23am

Hallucinations

I saw a skeleton.

Is this a sign?

I miss your voice.

I miss your touch.

I feel like I am drowning.

Please answer.

Teach me how to breathe again;

Teach me how to swim towards you.

I want you to feel the way I feel it.

The waves crashing against me.

Against my lungs.

I'm spiraling down

And I honestly don't know how to swim out of it.

11.01.15

8:14pm

Henry David Thoreau

They say paper is what keeps us living.

Money is a necessity in this life.

I deny it.

Go down to a river bend

& drink from its waters.

Build a shelter with the forest

& map your night out with the stars.

Create a spark among the stones,

Create a ripple within the shores.

01.09.15

10:04pm

Her.

Do you ever miss her?

Just imagine holding her,

Or turning on your side,

Knowing she would be

Smiling at you with them

Blue eyes and white smile

That all her love is just

Illuminating off her skin.

How you long to reach at

That light and tell her

That you can't believe

How she is yours.

11.01.15

8:16pm

Hesitation

My conscious stuck in November.

You're driving your pop's car,

One hand on the wheel,

Radio, on.

Every song sung was telling us to kiss.

I saw you peeking at me on your right.

My hand next to yours on the center console.

How much I just wanted you to take my hand into yours.

You broke our silence with an apology.

"Sorry I don't have much to say..."

I went to reply but you stole my voice,

"I just get lost for words when I look at you."

My face instantly hot.

I buried my face into my shoulder so you couldn't see me smile.

My heart pounded in my ears.

My thoughts shouting!

Your face then changed.

You looked sad?

Worried?

Oh no!

It’s because I didn’t say anything back!

Silence fell between us once more.

I am no longer hot.

I am cold.

Mad at myself for not responding.

I want to shout that I feel the same way!

I really do!

I lost my chance...

The radio still on.

Telling us to kiss once more.

But now both of his hands are on the wheel.

12.16.14

9:11pm

High School Daydream

I dream of kissing you but

I never kissed your lips.

I dream of loving you but

I never dare try.

See it's a fear of mine,

I don't know why.

Maybe you will think I'm crazy

Because I am waiting for

Someone who does not

Want to be wanted.

11.01.15

8:19pm

His/Her Thoughts

She had this way about her that made you feel alive.

He had this sweetness about him that made you feel safe.

Her laugh filled a room,

Her hair complemented her personality,

And her eyes reflected her smile.

His hands were strong,

His smile, shy,

And his expressions were goofy.

I had to resist to be close to her.

I had to resist to be close to him.

But at times I would sit so close that our thighs were touching!

But at a times he sat so close to me our thighs were touching!

She made me so nervous.

He made me so nervous.

One night, I kept catching her glance at my lips.

I couldn't tell if she knew I caught her,

But she would just flash her radiant smile my way.

One night, I kept glancing at his lips.

He caught me a few times.

I know he did, so I just smiled.

I usually made the first approach,

and I regret that I didn't that night.

There was no kiss.

Maybe he doesn't like me.

I couldn't make a move because she's different.

But he is different.

She's perfect.

So I wanted the kiss to be perfect.

Should I wait for him?

12.23.14

9:14pm

Holly

Curious cat just close your eyes.

I see you are tired,

But you watch what I write

As if you can read.

You extend a paw

And begin to write.

Curious cat you remind me of a child.

Clingy & innocent with big eyes.

06.06.16

11:19pm

How To Love?

I was a king without a queen,

Until I saw your face, worthy of a crown.

I struggled to reach you,

I knelt on one knee and asked you.

Your eyes lit up, but your face had a frown.

With a flick of the light, she was gone.

She didn't even turn back to say goodbye,

A faint whisper of her voice appeared,

"There is no one I can love,"

"Because I don't know how."

12.14.14

9:39pm

Hurtful Wishing

Yet again I must deny my desires for you.

To shun the feeling of love for the first time.

This time it is for nine months longer.

How can I go on when it is scratching the surface?

Do I dare itch?

Itch the feeling that you feel the same,

Or itch the feeling of hurtful wishing?

11.01.15

8:21PM

I Cannot Wait

I cannot wait to drive your car.

I cannot wait to be in your arms.

I cannot wait to see that smile.

I cannot wait to drive you wild.

I cannot wait to steal a kiss.

I cannot wait for complete bliss.

I cannot wait to live the dream

I've been dreaming of for a while.

12.16.14

9:04pm

I Wonder

I write to get my thoughts out.

Just like others before me have.

It may start a worldly revolution,

Or just between us two.

12.14.14

8:31pm

Immortality

We all think living forever would be great.

To be forever young.

For your friends,

They may not have chosen the same path.

You feel more alone,

And cold.

Don't make this wish.

Don't choose this.

12.16.14

8:54pm

Independent

Lately it seems like you are all I write.

I thank you for that.

If one day, they publish -

I hope you get to read.

For I will make millions,

Without your please.

12.14.14

8:27pm

Insomnia

I used to love her.

When I was young, she would take over.

But now,

Since I am wiser,

I do not want her to visit me no more.

She makes me stay up,

And think.

I just want to rest.

But when I can lay at rest,

It is the best I ever had.

12.16.14

8:28pm

Intro

She writes in the darkness
With only light casted
Still between her knees.

For this leave no distractions
Due to surroundings.

They have too long forsaken
Her thoughts that need
To be flown unto me.

11.01.15

8:26pm

J.C.

A married man

is not one to play.

The single way

is not his game.

To test out waters

he no longer sails.

To leave the woman

he sworn to stay.

12.16.14

9:42pm

K.I.A.

A loud noise next to his ears,
Ringing quickly appears.

His vision quivers,
His hands shake,
And his brain rattles.

Lieutenant yells to him,
"Get down!"
But someone shoots him
To the ground.

07.28.16

5:40am

L.

You been on my mind like a drug

Heaven help me if I’m in love.

04.05.16

8:31pm

L.C.

Words are easier flown unto thee.

Just like the easiness of love,

No matter how complicated we make it ought to be.

Because what I love I can never say.

Like your sweetness and caring soul for others.

By your look, and the way you look at me.

I fall every time for those twinkling eyes.

It lifts me up to our own little world.

Your smile, those lips, and the sound that comes from them.

Your arms wrapped around me instantly become my safe blanket.

Never wanting to unwrap your warmth.

Those hands,

Hard working, but gentle to my touch.

As I see this light inside you start to glow,

Your soul dances with mine.

The way the music flows through one another

Is unexplainable.

I don't want to see this in no one else.

It might sound selfish,

But call me greedy for wanting every second of your time.

For everything you wish, I wished a thousand times.

12.16.14

9:39pm

Last Call

Why do you call at closing time?

The doors are shut,

And so are my legs.

You say, “last call.”

I accept.

I accept.

I accept.

No more.

11.01.15

8:23pm

Letter

We give people so many chances to redeem themselves.

But only one letter can change the word love to love**d**.

12.14.14

8:18pm

Leukemia

I can't believe how fast your life could change.

How your health is at fault.

A checkup could become a death sentence,

It turns your world upside down.

Your breath is inhaled slowly,

But exhaled quickly.

The family is here for you

And we will do what we can for you to live the remainder of your life,

The way you want to.

12.14.14

8:22pm

Libra

His world moves too quick.

Mine burns too bright.

But he plays coy,

When I play rough.

There are times he takes control,

And the innocence of me comes out.

We are never equal,

But always balancing out.

12.16.14

9:09pm

Long Distance

Why do I love you?

You are nowhere near,

For I should not love you.

I should love ones here.

So please come home -

So I can invite you in.

07.28.16

5:28am

Lost In Chicago

What happens when he realizes I am no longer enough?

Or when he realizes that all my shattered pieces scrape him?

I cannot live with that.

I can't live without him.

I became lost tonight.

I let the wind take me in every direction.

I crossed streets I never have before.

I talked to anyone who would listen,

And only talked of you.

01.03.16

7:06pm

Love Making

I sat up against the wall connecting my bed.

I turned to look at you already watching me.

Smiling, you came closer

Until the center faded.

And so did the time spent between it.

Every second flourished.

Every breathe panted.

Eyes lock before they roll back.

Through the storm,

Thighs connected,

And centers sore.

11.01.15

8:24pm

Love The Irony

My eyes are as blue

As the oceans he sails on.

I surround you.

You chose the waves,

You chose the color,

The irony is sinking.

11.01.15

8:34pm

Loving A Sailor

A three hour wait to see him come off the ship. Even when you know he is on that ship, there is a doubt. But it leaves the second it knocked. His family cheering his name. They turn to me with tears and smiles. The youngest hugs me and laughs with joy.

Eighteen days come and go too quick. Time to board the ship once more. It's quiet. Not like the last. These tears are filled with don't go's and have to's. I watch him hug his family. I stand silent and still. My eyes wander to mothers and wives. I wonder if their lives are my future. Then I look at their whaling children. I look away and see him standing in front of me. He is holding back tears, but I let one fall. He wipes it and hugs me long. We exchange miss you's and love. His family watches with sadness and joy. He says one final goodbye and then boards the ship. We stay to watch the others board. The ship finally sets sail onto their next port.

We get in the car,

Everyone silent.

Everyone still.

Nine more months. Again and again and again.

06.08.16

11:50pm

Luna

The moon winks,

The moon moves,

Trying to fit between my blinds.

The moon breathes,

The moon shines,

Trying to catch my attention.

The moon smiles,

The moon stays.

Trying not to linger,

But I don't mind.

12.14.14

9:29pm

Lust

He is the kind who likes to play

The game that can make you feel sick.

Unless you are the one he plays for.

It is different when you are on the other side.

The one he plays for,

The other does not know.

For it is the woman at fault.

He gets away by her default.

He goes back to the woman and child.

But he lays in bed thinking of the one,

He desires to win.

12.16.14

8:58pm

Lyrics

Your name is the title of a song,

I cannot get it off repeat.

It is a constant replay

That is driving me insane.

The only thing different about this song,

Is that the lyrics were made out of the words -

That were never said.

11.01.15

8:26pm

Mother

Why do you hover?

He is young, yes, but he needs room to roam.

To spread his wings when it is time to go.

He will soon become a young man,

Chasing women in the streets.

He is now that young man.

He needs to go,

Why do you hover?

11.01.15

8:27pm

My Way Out

I wonder,

Do you daydream?

My daydreams are filled of you.

In a haunted house,

I walk through the darkness,

Searching.

Searching for a way out.

A breeze finds its way to my brow.

I turn around

And you push towards my face.

Followed by your embrace,

I finally found my way out of the darkness,

Out of this house.

01.03.16

7:04pm

Naked Delight

Seeing another body is exposure.

I let my hand caress you in the slightest of touches.

Such beautiful art in the curvature of your spine.

And such smooth edges around the harsh tightness of a scar.

I run my hand along your arm and some bumps stand out.

Those chills are the start button to your senses.

You catch my hand and turn to me.

Raising my hand to your heart,

You nod once to confirm, more.

06.08.16

11:23pm

Never Had

Sometimes I wake up to the sound of your voice,
Not knowing that it was only a dream until my senses kicked in.

Sometimes I see you with another,
Wondering if that's what it would look like if I were she.

Sometimes I think of what it would have been,
If we hadn't been so selfish.

Sometimes I forget the hurt,
But I never will forget that you were the best I never had.

11.01.15

8:27pm

Odd

Now it is my turn

To be the one with the broken heart.

I don't want this.

My heart aches,

For you,

And from what you did.

I used to be the one with power.

I guess giving it to you was okay.

Because for some reason I know I will be okay.

And I am content with this chapter being closed.

12.23.14

9:07pm

Only For One Night

Give into the night,

Give into me.

Just once.

One time to just let go.

Let all your desires flood unto me.

I'll keep you safe,

I'll take care of you.

Just remember,

It is only for one night.

11.01.15

8:32pm

Only One

Only one more drink.

Only one more touch.

Only one more kiss.

Only if it was with me.

None of it was for me.

For that one night,

If you did not take that last sip,

You would not have been with her.

You looked at me,

But still left with her.

Why her?

I thought you said I was the only one.

01.03.16

7:15pm

Out To Sea

You were my voice.
With it taken away
Like Ursula with her shell
You swim away farther from sea.
I am at bay with no words to say.

The worst cry is
Shouting,
Then silence.

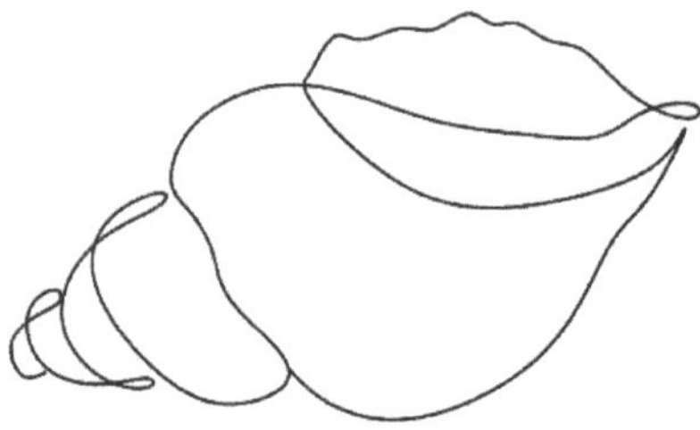

11.01.15

8:35pm

Parachute

I am looking down to those who look up at me.
I am a part of the skyline.
He brushes my hair from my neck.
Making me look up to the full moon.
His brings me to his mouth,
Drowning out all my thoughts.

I wanted this moment for so long,
And I know this is right.

Right now,
With him.

He presses against me and picks me up.
The glass window is ice to my bare skin.
I gasp at the crisp touch.
But his hunger warms me quickly.

07.28.16

5:39am

Plane To Vegas

Listening to Ella

Singing about love and needing to be yours.

I cry as I fly 1500 feet above

You back at home

Flipping through my thoughts, wishing all the words said, weren't.

I forgave the words said but can't seem to hit pause.

They play at random times throughout the day

Honestly, I will never forget what you said

And I will never forget that kind of hurt.

12.16.14

8:52pm

Rattle My Brain

I am with none in the night

because I wonder if you are.

If you have forgotten me

like I desperately try to do with you.

I cannot shake you off my brain,

so I try to rattle them unto page.

12.23.14

9:25pm

Re-Boot

I don't want to re-wire you.
The program can be the same.
But what have they done to you?
What have you seen?
What life are you forced to live,
To be so different?
To hate so much...
To feel unseen...

07.28.16

4:55am

Reading Your Hesitation

I watch you,

I can see your hesitation

but I wonder if it is because you see mine.

I am trying to figure you out

But you give me that look.

Your eyes capturing

and your lips parted.

I try not to linger

But it is hard not being where you are.

I want more than this friendship.

Just say the word

And I will let you into my world.

But that hesitation appears once more

And your lips,

No longer parted.

I linger a little while.

But you are the first to leave.

12.16.14

10:38pm

Red Light Special

She was upset.

Something her boyfriend did.

So she called me.

Her *friend.*

I picked her up and drove.

I waited for her to speak first,

Whenever she was ready.

She told me what happened and all I could say

Was that I would have never done that to her if I was him,

She stared at me in complete silence.

She wouldn't take her eyes off me,

And I wouldn't take my eyes off the road.

Waiting for her to unlock her gaze from me,

The next light turned red.

When I came to a stop,

She leaned in close,

And parted her lips unto mine.

11.01.15

8:42pm

Regret

When two people love each other

& don't say a word,

What is that called?

Fear?

No.

It is what I feel

Every night,

Alone.

12.16.14

9:59pm

Repaired

November quickens to cold

And so do my hands.

Another month of this bitter wind.

But the wind pushes you toward me.

So I try not to complain.

December is around the corner

And your plane will land soon after.

Funny how you will arrive on an object you fix.

A mechanic for the past nine months,

But it really is my heart you repaired.

The last piece I am waiting for,

Is you.

12.23.14

8:54pm

Sailing Away

It's okay.

Lock up those feelings and

Push my love away.

Remember,

You're sailing on waters

The color of my eyes.

12.16.14

9:02pm

Same Hurt in A Different Life

The world without us humans
Would be the same.
I would be a river,
Flowing to my love at the bend.
Only to find you
Spread among the others.

11.01.15

7:57pm

Scare

It wouldn't be yours,

Why'd I do that?

Because it felt great to be touched again?

It wasn't that long, was it?

I don't care.

You hurt me.

And I thought that would heal me.

Not numb my body,

And awaken my worry.

11.01.15

8:44pm

Seattle

You moved away from me.

I was waiting for you.

You couldn't do the same?

You don't think I feel alone?

My thoughts are painted with your smile,

And sorrow.

I did that.

I created both,

But I wish I could take it back.

I want you to forgive me,

to forget about it all.

I regret everything.

Don't you see I am dying inside!

All I want to do is open me up,

And show you all that is rotting away is me.

The only way I can survive is to know that you will not forget me.

11.01.15

8:45pm

Secrets At Dinner

The thirst to hear your voice is lethal.

So I talked to your mother.

She told me things I never knew.

That message filled me.

Through butterflies & shock.

She reassured my memories and even planted a few to sprout.

01.09.15

10:01pm

Shadow

You just know how to move.

How to twitch your brow and lips.

How to mirror my every step.

You consume me with every breath.

And know exactly what to say to make me melt.

12.16.14

10:50pm

She.

She is just enough of a challenge

so I don't get bored.

There is a bit of a chase

even once I have her.

She knows the game

I like to play.

Sometimes I just sit

and stare at her face.

She's reading.

I cannot believe how beautiful

her European features are.

She hates her nose,

but her hate drives me to love it.

Her fingers brush her forehead,

and my eyes flash to her figure.

I ask myself why I am not sitting next to her,

so I get up to hold her.

She stands up

& we sway on the carpet awhile.

I need to smell her,

to breathe her in.

Her air makes me high,

I cannot be any higher than this.

This is paradise,

She is my paradise.

And the only way I am ever going to come down,

Is on one knee.

04.05.16

8:18pm

Sleepover

I wasn't where I thought I was
Because when I turned my head
There you were, lying inches from my face.
My hand still intertwined with yours.
I stare for a while, and smile.
You start to wake to your natural alarm.
Seeing you open from the sand is a beautiful sight.
Your eyes so rested and so blue.
They rest on me, then match mine.
I whisper good morning in your hair
And you pull onto me tighter, closer.
I want to kiss your lips but I hesitate.
I second guess myself around you.
Holding onto this moment,
Holding onto this memory.
A memory that will be replaying on the drive home.
You never leave my mind.
Don't you dare leave my side.

12.16.14

9:24pm

Snow Days

Some days you need to be young again.

Not young for love,

Young with imagination.

Go outside and lay in the snow belly up.

Don't look through elder eyes,

But eyes that carry those fond memories of childhood laughter and playful manner.

12.16.14

9:38pm

Sophia

For I cannot think of that baby,

it reminds me of her.

For I cannot see the baby,

it is not mine.

For I cannot hold the baby,

it is not ours.

I know it is not the baby at fault,

but you.

12.16.14

9:17pm

Stupid Girl Chasing a Stupid Boy

There is nothing greater

than destination.

If my destination is where

you are.

Then why do you keep

changing it?

06.09.16

12:02am

T.N.

I dreamt of the night we met.

We reached up at the same time

And somehow our hands collided.

We stood there in awe

But now do I wish there were more than your eyes?

12.14.14

8:53pm

Temptation

20 years they been together.

But he looks away-

From the one he married,

To those who sway.

She does not see his eyes wander.

For she is never around,

But I am.

His eyes wander to me.

They are filled with lust and wonder.

I do not feel the same,

Or so I tell myself.

I am not this type of person.

For I am a lady,

One who obeys and respects the art of marriage.

But I cannot resist the touch

Of a taken man.

12.14.14

9:22pm

Temptation Knocks

Temptation knocks as his ring shines.

I hold my breath to not take in his scent.

For the sound of his song makes me blush,

“Me gusta sus ojos, su boca , su cuerpo , su todo.”

He takes my hand by surprise, twirling me into his body.

My eyes filled with sweetness,

As he leans in with eagerness.

Temptation knocks but I-

-pull away.

06.09.16

12:01am

The Book Thief

I never had a love this deep.

To the core of many living things,

It reminds me of my tears.

For they do not shed as much as they did

From death's perspective.

So I am her.

Denying the kisses

And missing those gone.

Because he was about to say it

But his breathe,

In the middle,

Was taken.

An unknown tragic

That I knew all too well.

02.21.15

10:30pm

The Day Before the Breakup

Is it okay that I am okay?

That I already accepted this fate?

That I only cry because I hurt for the future

For what's to come, or not.

More towards not.

Because you are the first love,

And for that, I don't want to love another.

I want you.

Whether I had a taste now and can get it back tomorrow.

Whether the taste now is bitter

And it only gets better with time,

But that time isn't for a couple years.

I can live with that.

I just don't want to live with nothing.

To go on without you.

Without any of you.

07.28.16

5:00am

The Human Torch

You say you hate to fight-

But you are the one that always ignites the flame.

11.01.15

8:51pm

The Key to Open My Heart

Believe me when I say I would not have it any other way. My life was built beyond walls and twenty years is what it took to take them down. You made me trust and more importantly, love. I never thought it was possible. Really, I didn't. It was weird and sudden, and unreal. It was never in my vocabulary. I felt warm, high, and whole. I don't even know what you did but I love it. I love that you helped me take the bricks down with you. You taught me to take my time, and to trust. And I guess I love that most about you. You are patient with me because you know it will make me stronger. You help me learn about myself and that it is okay to open these feelings. These feelings of understanding, hope, and love. The best part of opening your heart is that your eyes open too. You see so much more of the everyday things. Like fireworks are not just beautiful patriotic light shows, but every rocket is my heartbeat. Bursting with love and the finale of the show is my heartbeat whenever we kiss. So, I thank you for this love lesson. For I love you for it. And for every lesson after that. For you are the key that opened my heart.

12.23.14

9:00pm

The Mad Hatter

My advice,

Don't dwell,

Just do it.

Tell that person

You have been driven mad

At the thought.

That you are in

Love with them.

Your heart will be

At ease.

Your mind can get

Some rest.

No matter the reply,

They will always

Remember that you

Love them.

And the regret of

Knowing, will drive

Them equally mad.

12.23.14

9:33pm

The Only Goodbye She Knows

For all you know are up and gone

They left you here all alone

Their town. Now yours.

The closest one of all left no notice.

She stood up and went.

You found out from her lover.

And he was pissed.

But maybe that was all she knew.

11.01.15

8:57pm

The Stare

There is always that stare before a kiss.

Just some stares are different.

You're different.

And I can't tell if this is the stare.

And I don't want to lean in for a kiss

That is not meant to be there.

01.09.15

10:05pm

The Trampoline

"Can I tell you a secret?"

"Shoot."

"I write poetry."

"Really, since when?"

"Since when I realized the moment I fell in love with you."

11.01.15

8:57pm

The Unknown

So strangely beautiful it was,

Her fears so darkly written.

For there was a light in her voice.

So she decided to love.

Love him despite the love for herself.

She absorbed the thought of love

As children are absorbed by television.

Unknowingly.

11.01.15

8:57pm

The Unsent Written Letter

Dear Sailor,

I wish I kissed you in the picture show. Or at least let you know for how long I lingered a little longer than normal. I am not being quite fair to you or to myself but who cares? You are gone every nine months on repeat. For once I will not linger because I will not be there at all. Not even in your thoughts...

07.28.16

5:17am

Thinking Is Fatal

My thoughts are multiple hurricanes

Every direction I'm drowning in doubt.

In thoughts

In hideaways.

Can you hear me when I say I need your shelter?

I have never felt this way.

Everything out of my control.

Everything is going left

Everything is going wrong.

I need the world to stop passing by with chaos.

I need this storm to pass,

To wash away every negative thought or action.

To wash away the tears and lonely nights

In my chaos

In my fears.

11.01.15

8:58pm

Thirst

It's like I'm living a life with no water

And you're the only one that can clench my thirst.

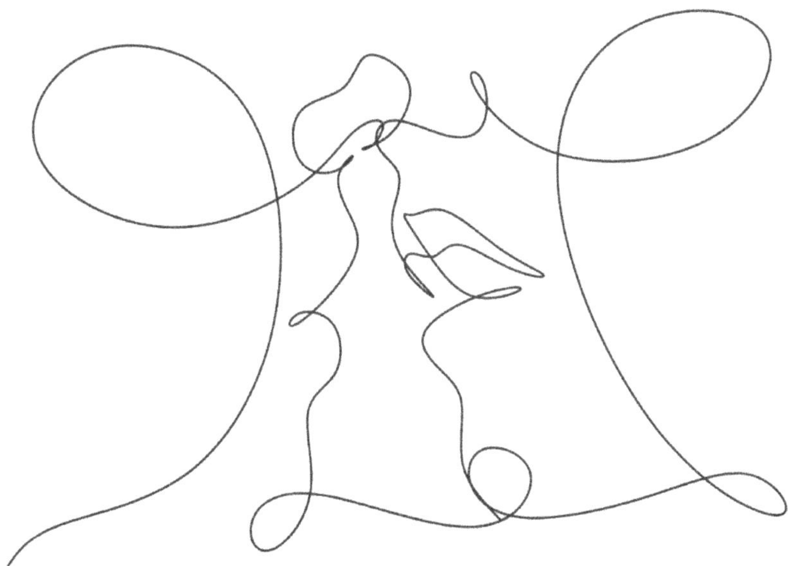

12.14.14

9:55pm

Those Like Me

When I think of you, I think of that night on the trampoline.

When I think of us, I smile stupidly.

After,

I realize this smile fades too quick.

For I am a realist,

And feelings do no good for those like me.

07.28.16

5:30am

Thoughts After an Argument

My worst fear is you.

To lose you for good every time you walk away

That one morning you don't come home.

All your things are gone for good.

Sometimes I wish I could just pause,

And think,

Before something is done or said

In order to lose you for good.

11.01.15

8:58pm

Trust Fall

I hope he is falling

Because I have been ready to catch him.

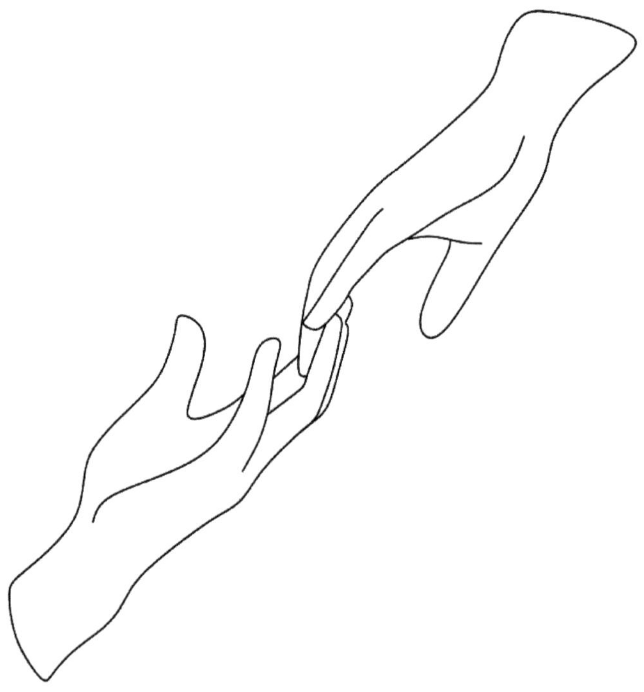

06.09.16

12:07am

Two Birds, One Stone

You told me maybe this was lust.

Maybe we were getting into something too quick.

I told you this was love and distance.

I told you what you were getting yourself into.

You said you could handle it.

You said you loved me.

She didn't look anything like me.

Why are you weak like him?

Like the one before you…

You said you'd never become him.

You said you'd never have been like him before.

But with the time passing you became just like him.

12.16.14

9:13pm

Unknown Promises

I promised myself to wait for you.

I never promised you.

So now I am scared.

For in your heart, I could be no one to you.

But in mine,

I am in love.

11.01.15

8:59pm

Unseen Love

How do you love a man you never see?

The kind who fights for our country overseas?

It scares me of what you can become,

A different sort of some.

I don't want to reprogram you,

I just want to love you.

The one I fell in love with

Before this deployment.

Before the sign.

Before the ink.

11.01.15

7:41pm

Used To

That's what it was.

I was so used to playing God

That when I got hurt,

It reminded me that I am human.

12.16.14

9:04pm

War

We are both fighting battles.

One is in my heart,

And the other is in Iraq.

12.16.14

8:55pm

Weak

Why are you my every thought?

I did not ask for this.

BE GONE!

Unless you are willing to stay...

11.01.15

7:47pm

What A Girl Wants

What do I want?

I want to find someone; to love someone.

And to be devoted to each other.

I want zero secrets and 110% trust, loyalty, and pick me ups.

Just to be bare with someone,

Not with our skin but mentally.

To strip down all those walls and just have complete acceptance.

That would be beautiful.

That is all I will ever want.

06.09.16

12:09am

What If

How I long to see you again.

The days are short,

The nights are never ending.

What if.

My heart aches.

My thoughts turn,

What if.

My lips thirst,

My body yearns,

But it can't.

What if.

11.01.15

9:01pm

What Keeps You?

I just want to feel you holding me.
Whispering that you love me,
That I am beautiful,
And that everything is going to be okay.
But when I am having a bad day
It just gets worse.
I think of you no longer here.
I just don't want to feel.
I try to hide from my thoughts
Under pillows and blankets.
The weight of them makes me drift into a 3 day slumber.

12.14.14

10:01pm

Witchcraft Isn't Real

There is a spell you put me under

Though I do not mind it,

I am scared.

For I never felt this way.

This spell is deadly, but I don't care.

What?

No spell?

So, you're telling me I made this choice...?

12.16.14

9:15pm

Wrong Bitch

The unknowing is a bitch.

When is her sister Karma going to turn around?

I would like to know something right about now.

What?

Did you think all Karma was…Was a bitch?

11.01.15

9:02pm

You Are My Routine

I feel lost if I don't talk to you.

You are a part of my routine.

*Stay tuned for future writings.

*If you would like to be featured in my future writings, purchase my poetry, subscribe to my email, and please leave a good review.

*Email me an experience or memory you hold close to you. Give me as much detail as possible.

*I will then reach out to you when you will be featured in the next book.

*Sign up at asbpoetry.com and see disclaimer.

A.S.B.

www.ingramcontent.com/pod-product-compliance
Ingram Content Group UK Ltd.
Pitfield, Milton Keynes, MK11 3LW, UK
UKHW020423250726
13967UKWH00007B/2791

9 780578 388465